The Champion In You

Adonis "Sporty" Jeralds

xulon
PRESS

Xulon Press
10640 Main Street
Suite 800
Fairfax, VA 22030
(703) 279-6511
XulonPress.com

Dedication

To my father Nick Jeralds.
You were always and continue to
be the "Wind Beneath My Wings."

To my mother JoAnn Jeralds.
Thank you for being my guiding light.

To Teresa, Jazmine and Jacob.
Thank you for your love.

Table of Contents

Acknowledgments

I would like to thank Johnny Harris, Steve Luquire, M.L. Carr, Tony Womack and John C. Lee, IV for their endorsement and support of this book; Crishon Jordan, who served as my editor throughout this project—her writing talents will some day produce a best seller; Philip Tate and Heather Naper for their thorough proofreading of this book; Andy Greenwell, George Wallace, and Steve Camp for believing in me; Ike Walker and Jack Jensen for showing me that champions are not necessarily measured by wins or losses; Ereka Crawford and Dustin Peck for their help with the cover design; all my colleagues at the Auditorium-Coliseum-Convention Center Authority and Hampton Coliseum; and my family and friends who have been so supportive of this project. May God Bless You.

—Sporty Jeralds

Introduction

The Champion In You is the culmination of a long journey that began with my desire to help people. This simple book contains advice on business, goal setting, community service and achieving excellence. Each short vignette is designed to challenge the reader to think beyond the words on the page and reflect on the true meaning of each one. For example, one of my favorites, "It's A J Not A G" speaks of my frustration with people who misspell my last name with a G. Although the vignette speaks directly to the point, the deeper message is attention to detail—making sure you do the little things that can and often do make the big difference.

We define champions by the victories they've won. My definition of a champion is a little different. I believe a champion is someone who uses the talent he has to the best of his ability, and in doing so makes the world a better place. Based on that definition all of us can be champions. I encourage you to read and reread this book. Ultimately my one desire through writing it is so that you may find the "Champion In You."

If

For all sad words of tongue or pen the saddest are these. It might have been!

John Greenleaf Whittier

"**I**f," it is often said, is the biggest word in the English language. Nearly all of us have used it at one time or another to describe what we think would make our lives better. That's because it is human nature to believe that things would be better if we were another person in another place.

For those not familiar with Russell Conwell's story "Acres of Diamonds," the tale is about an African farmer whose land was very rocky and difficult to till. The farmer hated working so hard for such small wages and believed he could find "easy wealth." Thus, he sold his farm in hopes of mining diamonds in the countryside. The man who bought the farmer's land soon found that the rocks on the

1

land were actually diamonds—acres and acres of diamonds. Meanwhile, the farmer who sold the property never found his diamonds and died poor. The moral of the story is that the farmer had riches well within his reach if only he had worked to find them.

Unfortunately, we cannot change the decisions we've made in the past. However, we can change our attitude from this day forward. Let us not be like the farmer, searching for dreams in far away places. If we commit right now to do the best we can with what we have, we will find "Acres of Diamonds" right under our noses.

Remember: Only you can use the talent you have.

Don't Vegetate...
Educate

Average is your enemy.

Pearce "Rocky" Lane

With satellite television and the availability of 500 channels, there is never a time when you cannot find something to watch. The question is whether or not the programming is worth watching.

Undoubtedly, watching television is one of the biggest obstacles on the path of those trying to reach their goals. Through reading, cultural programs, seminars and classes that in many cases are absolutely free, we can educate ourselves and maintain an edge over our contemporaries. Yet, most people are content to come home after work and vegetate in front of their television. In fact, Americans watch over 20 hours of TV per week. That's 20 hours they could spend on more enriching activities such as exercise, reading, hobbies, family interaction, volunteering for charitable organizations—the list is endless.

Start today by making a commitment to watch no more than one hour of television per day. Invest the other hours in personal development. You'll be amazed at how much you can accomplish each day and soon discover that you don't miss those channels as much as you thought you would.

Remember: You can always watch reruns, but you never get a second chance to relive a day.

Solid As A Rock

If you have built castles in the air, your work need not be lost; that is where they should be. Now put foundations under them.

Thoreau

Several years ago there was a national advertising campaign entitled, "Reading Is Fundamental." The campaign was designed to emphasize that reading was fundamental to the educational process, providing the foundation on which all other learning was built. The key in this campaign was the strength of the foundation.

The same is true in construction. A structure must be built on a solid foundation. The foundation provides the stability needed for the structure to endure and stand the test of time. It doesn't matter how good the materials are in the rest of the structure. If the foundation is not solidly constructed, the house will not last.

Roland Hemond, who as general manager helped build the Baltimore Orioles into a very successful franchise, spoke of how champions are made. "Show me a championship team and I'll show you one who has mastered the fundamentals—the little things that often spell the difference between winning and losing. Countless players who have the material requisites for greatness—still fail. Why? Because they can't master the basics. Learning the fundamentals is essential in sports and business."

Michael Jordan devotes a whole chapter of his book, "I Can't Accept Not Trying" to mastering the fundamentals. He credits much of his success to having learned the fundamentals early in his career at the University of North Carolina-Chapel Hill. He believes very firmly that mastering the fundamentals are important to any endeavor. He states, "the fundamentals are the building blocks or principles that make everything work. I don't care what you're doing or what you're trying to accomplish; you can't skip the fundamentals if you want to be the best. The minute you get away from the fundamentals the bottom can fall out of your game, your schoolwork, your job, whatever you are doing." He even compliments another great player, Larry Bird. Jordan states, "He essentially mastered the fundamentals to the point that he overcame any physical limitations he might have had."

If a successful career in a particular field is your ultimate goal, build your foundation on the fundamentals.

Remember: If you spend too much time learning the tricks of the trade, you may never learn the trade.

No Fear

You gain strength, courage and confidence by every experience in which you really stop to look fear in the face. You must do the thing you think you cannot do.

Eleanor Roosevelt

It's hard to believe, but studies have shown that Americans fear speaking in public more than dying. I once was one of those people. I can remember having to make a presentation before members of my graduate school class as a 22-year-old. Although I had performed in athletic contests in front of thousands problem-free, the prospect of speaking before fifteen of my peers kept me from sleeping the night before my presentation. Somehow I got through it, but I know it was not a good showing.

Shortly after being hired for my first "real" job, I was placed in the terrifying position of having to speak before an audience of over 200. My boss and several other high ranking city officials unanimously nominated me to be the master of ceremonies at a luncheon. I knew I could not decline this invitation. As uncomfortable as it made me feel, their support gave me the confidence to accept what, for me, was a very big challenge. I decided my best chance to do well was to be as prepared as possible. I practiced everyday for a month in front of a mirror. I incorporated some sure-fire humor, which I knew would loosen things up for me and the audience. The preparation paid off. On the big day I was nervous, but felt comfortable when I started the program. I even received a few compliments after it was over.

I faced one of my biggest fears and lived to tell about it. That luncheon proved to be a defining moment in my career. Over the years I have spoken before audiences as diverse as 1200 middle school students to a group of five at a local church. Obviously, I'm still a little nervous but I've come to realize that preparing each time allows me to convey my message with passion and confidence.

What is your biggest fear? What could you do today to conquer that fear? Whether it's public speaking, computer software applications or analyzing financial statements, there are steps you can take and people who can help you conquer your fears. To realize your full potential you must, at some point, conquer your fears.

Michael Johnson, Olympic Gold Medalist stated it this way. "After you have stared long enough into the dragons eyes, there is nothing left to do but slay the dragon."

Remember: All we have to fear is fear itself.

Franklin D Roosevelt

Get Fired Up

The secret of happiness is not in doing what one likes, but in liking what one does.

James M. Barrie

When you think of spark plugs, you probably think of those small automobile parts that fire up an engine. But another definition of a spark plug is something that initiates or gives impetus to an undertaking. If you are to be truly successful, you must find your spark plug, that is, the one thing that revs up your personal engine and gets you excited about going to work that day.

Personally, my life has been sparked by two things—my love for sports and my love of public service. I come from a long line of public servants, and truly enjoy making a difference in the lives of others. Through my master's degrees I was able to unite my two spark plugs within the field of public facilities management. Although I had no idea what I wanted to study in college, having the knowledge that my career needed to involve public service and sports allowed me to direct my energies toward a job that would encompass those two general areas.

Often, I speak with college graduates who really haven't decided what they want to do in life. I challenge them to find that spark plug. Perhaps you've always had a love for animals. Well become a veterinarian, work at the zoo or volunteer at the humane society. Perhaps you have a love for airplanes. Then become an air traffic controller, airport manager, flight attendant or even a pilot. The bottom line is to find something that will make you happy. I am convinced that the following equation is critical to becoming successful.

If you find a job doing something or being involved with something you love, then:
You will *do* a good job.
You will *be recognized* for doing a good job.
You will *get promoted* and make a *good* living.

Remember: Find out what puts the spark in your life.

Championship Pointers

The best prize life offers is the chance to work hard at work worth doing.

Find out what you love to do and you will never have to work another day in your life.

To love what you *do* and feel that it matters—how could anything be more fun.

A man who is born with a talent which he was meant to use finds his greatest happiness in using it.

The Dog Ate My Homework

The circumstances that surround a man's life are not important. How that man responds to those circumstances is important. His response is the ultimate determining factor between success and failure.

Booker T. Washington

Remember when the teacher asked for homework assignments. She'd get some pretty creative excuses. The power was out, my little brother tore it up, the dog ate it. Although allowing your dog to eat your homework would actually be embarrassing, we have been conditioned to think that would be better than telling the teacher you just didn't do your work. Ironically, the teacher would probably appreciate you telling the truth and be more lenient than if you made excuses.

Unfortunately, far too many people continue to rely on excuses throughout their childhood and adult lives. They blame being late for work on their children. They blame missed promotions on fellow employees. They blame credit problems on the economy. In short, they blame their problems on others and accept no responsibility for themselves.

My college basketball coach used to say, **"Bring back results and not excuses."** As a manager, parent, mentor or friend, I encourage people to bring me results or at least spare me the excuses. If you are late for work, don't blame the children. Allow enough time to get them to school and yourself to the job on time. Don't blame the missed promotion on a co-worker. Examine yourself and realize that maybe you have not prepared, studied or worked hard enough for that promotion. Don't allow your children to blame the teacher for their bad grades when you know their own behavior is disruptive.

Michael Jackson had a hit song years ago about each individual taking responsibility for him or herself. It was appropriately entitled, **"Man In The Mirror."** Let us all look in the mirror and realize that we are the masters of our own fate.

Remember: Why waste time inventing an excuse when you can create a solution.

Get Physical

He who has health has hope; and he who has hope has everything.

O ne of the things that amazes me when I talk with young professionals is that very few give any thought to preventative health maintenance. Spurred by a history of high blood pressure in my family, I have a comprehensive physical examination once a year. Yet I'm sure the average American spends more time and money on preventative maintenance of an automobile than on his or her body.

These are some of the reasons I hear from people for not visiting the doctor before they get sick. 1. **I don't have time**. But, do you have time to take an extended amount of time off work after you get sick? 2. **Doctors visits cost too much**. You can't put a price on good health. Think of the cost if you develop a serious problem that could have been diagnosed early, and treated or prevented. 3. **I feel**

fine. All the more reason to reconfirm you are healthy for another year. 4. **I'm afraid of what the doctor might find.** With the advances in medicine there are very few illnesses that cannot be cured, but early detection is the key to survival. The bottom line is there is no good reason for not visiting the doctor on an annual basis.

Make an appointment today for your physical examination. Just as preventative maintenance can help your automobile last years longer, the investment in preventative maintenance for your body will keep it running smoothly for a long time.

I suggest you find a young doctor. Why young? Because you'll want to grow old with your doctor.

Remember: Take care of your body, and it will take care of you.

Rest Assured

Fatigue makes cowards of us all.

Ever wonder why small children always have so much energy. One big reason is they always get their rest. Sleeping eight to ten hours per night would most assuredly boost your energy levels.

Dr. James Mass, author of *Power Sleep* states that, "100 million Americans are moderately to severely sleep deprived. So much so that it spoils their productivity, their relationships with their spouses and their kids. Twenty-five percent of the workforces are shift workers; fifty-six percent of shift workers fall asleep on the job at least once a week. Nearly every high school and college student is a walking zombie. And 40 million Americans have one or more sleep disorders. This is costing America 100 billion annually in terms of productivity, illness, absences and even death."

It's interesting how the information above referenced high school and college students. The question is at what point do parents allow their children to make up their own minds on what is an appropriate hour for bed. It seems likely that a midnight curfew in high school easily becomes 1 or 2 am in college. With a great deal of emphasis on partying, which in many cases is not just limited to the weekends, students get into the terrible habit of sleeping just a few hours nightly. Unfortunately, once they begin their first full time job, they find it very difficult to break the cycle.

As a manager, I see the yawns in meetings, the edginess of employees after an all night changeover and the illnesses that seem to affect otherwise healthy individuals. All of these are indicators of sleep deprivation.

Sleep is the vehicle by which we are allowed to rejuvenate ourselves physically and mentally. With rare exception there are few of us who can consistently perform at peak performance levels without adequate sleep. The average adult needs between 6 and 8 hours of sleep per night to function at maximum productivity. If you are not approaching these levels it's a good time to adjust your schedule accordingly. Although you may not quite have the energy of a 4 or 5 year old, you are guaranteed to be fresher than your contemporaries are.

Remember: Never underestimate the power of a good night's sleep.

Which Came First?

A man who does not read good books has no advantage over a man who can't read them.

A question that can generate a great deal of discussion among people is, "which came first, the chicken or the egg?" I've thought about that question and I surely don't have the answer.

I was reminded of the chicken and egg question recently when I heard a motivational speaker make the statement that the overwhelming majority of the homes in this country valued at over $200,000 have a library in them. I thought about the half dozen or so homes in that price range that I have visited and all of them had libraries. I asked myself, did they assemble a library to compliment their expensive home or did they have the books that now compose their library long before they had a nice home? I would say that in all cases these successful people had some semblance of a library in their first apartment.

It was Charlie "Tremendous" Jones who said, "Readers Are Leaders." The legendary basketball coach John Wooden once said, "We should drink from good books everyday."

Although I have a modest home now, I have a substantial collection of books contained in my den. I am confident that when I build my dream home (notice I didn't say if), it will contain a library.

Certainly in the future, as inflation rises, a $200,000 home could be considered modest and maybe then the benchmark for homes with libraries may be $500,000. The bottom line is quite simple—**most successful people read extensively**.

One of the things you can do right now to boost your career is to start a library in your home or apartment. Shop around. You can get some great deals on used and new books. If you have an apartment and limited space, give away some of those clothes you haven't worn in five years and use a closet for your library.

Start your library today and read. Maybe one day you'll invite me over to your big, pretty $500,000 home.

Remember: Either read or learn to fail gracefully.

Split Second

Many are called, few are chosen.

Anonymous

One of the innovations that the Dallas Cowboys brought to major league sports was the recruitment of athletes from sports other than football. After my senior basketball season, a teammate and I were evaluated by the Cowboys with the possibility of being invited to training camp as free agents.

First, we were given a written examination to test our general aptitude. I scored slightly better on those tests than my teammate. Next, we were given a series of agility tests. Both of us scored well on those. Finally, we ran a 40-yard dash to test our speed, not realizing that the standard by which we were being judged was 4.5 seconds. My teammate ran a 4.49, and I ran a 4.6. My teammate received an invitation to training camp, and I received a Dallas Cowboys ink pen.

Looking back at that experience I believe the only true test was the 40-yard dash. Because the Cowboys evaluated so many athletes, it was easiest to use the 40-yard dash speed as the ultimate determining factor on who would be invited to training camp. Naturally, I was disappointed to realize that one tenth of a second cost me an opportunity to be evaluated with the other players. If I had known 4.5 seconds was the goal, I could have trained to make that speed.

This experience serves as a good parable for life. The smallest amount of extra effort is the difference between winning and being an "also ran." The willingness to undertake an extra assignment, working on Saturday or Sunday or attending training sessions or extra classes can make the difference between getting that promotion or raise and just being an average employee.

The difference between my experience with the Cowboys and you being successful in your career is that you know what it takes to make it. Talent combined with hard work will ensure your success.

Remember: The only difference between ordinary and extraordinary is that little "extra."

Where You Think You Going?

Some of us aren't prepared to accept success—especially someone else's.

Sarah Vaughn

While living in the Tidewater area of Virginia, I learned the unique art of "crabbing." Crabbing, quite simply, is catching crabs. The easiest way to catch these tasty creatures is to attach some raw chicken to a string about 15 to 20 feet long and throw it into the water. Within a couple of minutes, you'll feel a tug on the end of the string. You very slowly pull the string in, and use a net to pick the crab from the water.

Although I love the taste of crabs, I always felt guilty about taking them home and allowing my wife to boil them. Part of this guilt lies in the fact that crabs seem to operate on the philosophy that they will all perish together. If you've ever seen crabs in a pot about to be boiled, you'll see that if one is able to make it to the top and seemingly escape, the others will pull him back into the pot so that they can all be boiled together.

We must always be on guard for those people who exhibit "crab" mentality because they will try to steal your dreams. As you climb the ladder of success and begin to leave these people behind, they will do everything they can to pull you down.

Don't let people destroy what you have worked for. Make a commitment to climb the ladder, and, if these people have been supportive of your endeavors, you can choose to reach back and pull them up with you.

Remember: Don't let others get you down.

Don't Listen To Your Critics

It's not the critic who counts, not the man who points out how the strong man stumbled, or where the doer of deeds could have done them better.

The credit belongs to the man who is actually in the arena; whose face is marred by dust and sweat and blood; who strives valiantly; who errs and comes short again and again; who knows the great enthusiasms, the great devotions, and spends himself in a worthy cause; who, at best, knows in the end the triumph of high achievement; and who, at the worst, if he fails, at least fails while daring greatly, so that his place shall never be with those cold and timid souls who know neither victory not defeat.

Theodore Roosevelt

You Don't Remember Me

You can get everything in life you want if you'll just help enough other people get what they want.

Zig Ziglar

We all know the importance of education and its value in our society. As we begin the 21st century it is quite evident those without at least a high school diploma will be left behind. Communities In Schools is an organization that works to stem the tide of students dropping out before completing high school. I love supporting this organization because I can see they are truly making a difference in our country.

At an annual awards luncheon I was excited to hear their keynote speaker Dorie Sanders. Ms. Sanders wrote the novel, "Clover." Her story is quite interesting in that she didn't write Clover until she was 55 years old and didn't have any previous literary experience. Ms. Sanders had copies of her book available for sale after the luncheon and was gracious enough to stay and autograph copies. Although I very rarely read novels, after hearing her speak I could not pass up the opportunity to meet her and have an autographed copy of her book.

As a courtesy, when I approached her in line I wrote my name in large letters on the back of my business card. As she was signing my book she said, "Sporty Jeralds, what a great name that would be for the dust cover of a book. I want to see your name on a book in the near future." I shall never forget those words because her words motivated me to write this book.

That encounter reminded me of something a member of the audience told me after hearing one of my **SUPER-HERO** speeches. That young man said to me, "you never know when you make a memory."

When you think about the power we all have to make a difference in someone else's life, it is important in personal encounters that we try to say something positive or uplifting or perform some act of kindness. What could be better than someday having a total stranger come up to you and say, "you don't remember me but ten years ago your words or act of kindness made a big difference in my life."

Remember: Only a life lived for others is worth living.

No Minimum Required

The difference between the right word and the almost right word is the difference between lightning and the lightning bug.

M ost of us remember an English composition class from high school or college. We were overwhelmed by some of the assignments—some of which required as many as 10 typewritten pages. We remember wondering how we could write enough for 10 typed pages? We remember feeling that we had thoroughly covered the subject with the first five or six pages and adding useless filler to make our 10 page minimum. Unfortunately, those English composition classes offered little in the way of help with business writing.

I had a great professor in graduate school who totally deprogrammed my thinking and taught me a valuable lesson that has helped me enormously in my career. His credo was *"clear, concise and free of ambiguity."* That saying will be indelibly inscribed in my mind. His requirement that we write several reports a week in that manner allowed me to write business memos very effectively in my first real job. The premise behind clear, concise and free of ambiguity is quite simple. **Business professionals are very busy; therefore, it is important that you say what you need to say in as few words as possible.** Luckily, there are no minimum requirements on the length of an effective memo. You may only need two lines to cover your subject. If that is the case, then just use two lines.

One of the things I do with all my written correspondence is to prepare a clean typewritten draft and then read it several times. The first check is for **spelling**. The next check is for **grammatical** errors. My final check is for **unnecessary words**. For example, instead of closing a letter by saying "if you have any questions after reviewing this memo, don't hesitate to call me." Just say, "please call if you have any questions." You have conveyed the same thought and used half the words. Take your business writing seriously, it is an important component of progressing up the career ladder.

Remember: Less is more.

What Did He Just Say?

Don't ever believe that the message has to be complicated to be effective.

Dr. Steve Franklin

After a great round of golf one Monday morning, I met the son of the golf pro in the clubhouse. I'd met him about a week earlier at one of the NBA games. This ten-year-old seemed pretty smart. I asked why he was not in school and he replied, "we had veterinarians day off." Actually, it was Veterans Day. I laughed to myself and, although it was pretty funny, I did not share his mistake with anyone else.

My response was pretty typical of how we behave when a child uses a word improperly or the wrong word. Unfortunately, when it is an adult in a professional situation it is no laughing matter. The words we use tell others many things about us. They convey one of two messages. Either this person is educated or really doesn't know what he or she is talking about. As is the case with most things—the simpler the better. Normal conversation between educated adults is built on the correct use of ordinary words.

Through the normal course of formal education we learn most of the words we would ever need to use. However, if you want to be more professional with your business communications it is important to continually expand your vocabulary. Probably, the most effective way to increase your vocabulary is through reading. Books, magazines and newspapers not only expose us to new words, they show how words are used appropriately. Daily reading will dramatically increase your vocabulary in a short period of time. Make a commitment to making your conversations no more complicated than they have to be.

Remember: KISS—Keep It Simple Stupid

Day By Day

By the mile it's a trial, by the yard it's hard; by the inch it's a cinch

What if you were presented with the challenge of losing 10 pounds? Or perhaps you were challenged to develop a strategic business plan for a new company, or learn a foreign language? You would receive no monetary reward for accomplishing this goal, but you would experience the satisfaction of accomplishing something you had always wanted to do.

Now suppose in order to help you lose 10 pounds you were locked in a health and fitness club for 13 days with the most advanced exercise equipment and three balanced meals each day. To help you draft your business plan you would be locked in the library for 13 days with the most current business books and periodicals. And to help you learn a new language you would be locked in a comfortable, isolated room for 13 days with the best instructional video and audio tapes. No doubt you could accomplish all of these goals under such extreme circumstances.

As much as the latest exercise equipment, business materials and instructional tapes would help you successfully reach these goals, probably the most important element is the difference 13 uninterrupted days would make.

Of course, most of us do not have 13 days we can devote to accomplishing our goals, but we could devote one hour a day, six days a week. While an hour may not seem like much time, six hours per week multiplied by 52 week equals 312 hours. Three hundred and twelve hours equals 13 days.

I have a personal goal of reading 25 books per year. Instead of sporadically trying to accomplish this goal, I try to dedicate an hour each night to reading. That way my goal of 25 new books broken down into daily doses becomes much easier to achieve.

There are few goals you cannot accomplish by dedicating 312 annual hours to them. If you want to realize your dreams, spend an hour or two a day working on them. You'll be surprised at the results that consistent daily effort will produce.

Remember: If you reach for your goals one hour at a time, they'll soon be within your grasp.

Say Good Words

Good words are worth much, and cost little.

Clara Hale, affectionately referred to as Mother Hale, is a lady from New York who cared for over 600 children—black, white and Hispanic—between the ages of two weeks and three years and who were addicted to drugs. These babies eventually overcame their drug addictions through the care offered by the Hale House. Mother Hale once said, "I hold them and rock them. They love for you to tell them how great they are, how good they are. Somehow, even at a young age they understand that."

The University of North Carolina Tar Heel Basketball team is another fine example of the power of good words. When a player comes out of the game, everybody on the bench stands and applauds that player. It doesn't matter if the player performed poorly—he still receives a standing ovation and encouraging words from his teammates. What an ideal place to play basketball—in an environment where everyone encourages you to do your best.

Even animals are believed to say "good words." Canadian geese, for example, fly in "V" formation during migration. The geese regularly change the leadership of the "V" because the lead goose, in fighting the headwind, helps create a partial vacuum for the geese on his right and left wings. Scientists have discovered in wind tunnel tests that the flock can fly 72 percent farther than an individual goose. It is also believed that when the geese honk, they are actually offering encouragement to each other, particularly to the lead goose.

Obviously the power of words is remarkable. As spouses, parents, brothers, sisters, supervisors, teachers and friends it is important that we say good words to the people whose lives we touch. Make it a habit to say something nice to the people you come in contact with on a daily basis. Even complete strangers appreciate a kind word from you. You'll be surprised at the difference you'll make in the lives of others and more importantly, at the difference you'll make in your own life.

Remember: Always put in a good word.

I Know Something Good About You

Wouldn't this old world be better
If the folks we meet would say
I know something good about you
And treat us just that way

Wouldn't it be fine and dandy
If a handshake warm and true
Carried with it this assurance
I know something good about you

Wouldn't things here be more pleasant
If the good that's in us all
Were the only things about us
That folks bothered to recall

Wouldn't life be lots more happy
If we praise the good we see
For there's such a lot of goodness
In the worst of you and me
Wouldn't it be nice to practice
This fine way of thinking, too
You know something good about me
I know something good about YOU

By All Means Persist

"Nothing in the world can take the place of persistence. Talent will not; nothing is more common than unsuccessful men with talent. Genius will not; unrewarded genius is almost a proverb. Education will not; the world is full of educated derelicts. Persistence and determination alone are omnipotent."

Calvin Coolidge

Studies of highly successful people reveal several characteristics that they all share. One of those characteristics is persistence. Rarely is it possible to be successful without persistence. The following story illustrates this point, and I frequently share it with young people who ask me about employment.

One day, a young lady named Ereka called me to explain that she had just finished college and wanted a job in the facilities management industry. She made it clear that she would work without pay in order to gain some industry experience. I told to her that we didn't have any available positions, but I would keep her in mind. About a month later, she called again reiterating her interest in facilities management. Again, I noted that we had no positions and appreciated her call. One month later, Ereka called with her same request for a small opportunity. While we still had no openings, I agreed to meet with her.

When I actually met her and saw her determination, I created an unpaid internship in our Marketing Department for her. She worked with us all day, and then worked at a drug store at night for income. After a few months, we starting paying her, and when a vacancy became available in her department, she was the first choice for the position. Successful people appreciate persistence in others because, in most cases, they had to persist in order to achieve their own goals and dreams.

Remember: If you are to reach your dreams, you must be willing to persist when others doubt you and sometimes when you doubt yourself.

The Rich Get Richer

Use it or lose it.

There is a biblical parable in the book of Matthew that conveys an important message. The story is about a master who leaves on a journey. Before he leaves, he calls three of his servants and gives money to each of them. To the first he gives five thousand dollars. To the second he gives two thousand dollars. To the third he gives one thousand dollars. The first servant invests his money wisely and gains five thousand dollars more. The second also uses his money wisely, doubling his investment. The third servant digs a hole and buries his money.

When the master returns, he is anxious to see what has become of his money. He is pleased that the first servant made an additional five thousand dollars and the second servant has also doubled his money. To both of them he said, "well done my good and faithful servant. You have been faithful over a few things; I will put you in charge of many things."

Upon realizing the third servant did nothing more than bury his money, the master is very disappointed. He said to him, "you lazy servant, you should have deposited my money with the bankers so that when I returned I would have received it back with interest." He then took the one thousand from him and gave it to the first servant. Finally he said, "for everyone who has will be given more and he will have abundance. Whoever does not have, even what he has will be taken from him."

The parable is one of my favorites because the theme is that we all have been entrusted with certain talents. As with the story, this does not mean that we all have the same amount of talent, but we all have talents nonetheless. In order to please God, we must use those talents. If we do, we will be blessed with even more. If, on the other hand, we decide to bury them, God will strip them from us. Starting today, make a commitment to yourself and God to use the talents he has bestowed upon you.

Remember: Make your master proud.

Do The Right Thing

It's never the wrong time to do the right thing.

One of my mother's favorite sayings when I was a child was "You know better than that." Now as a parent I constantly hear myself repeating that same phrase to my son and daughter.

As most parents know, once your baby turns into a toddler all the rules change. The ability to walk turns a once precious baby into a prisoner and parents into wardens. One day while in the kitchen, I took my eye off my then nine month old son for a few seconds and he touched the hot oven. Quickly he drew his fingers back and began to cry madly. Once I realized what happened, I picked him up and comforted him until he quieted down. To make sure the incident didn't happen again, I placed him in front of the oven, touched it with my finger, pulled my finger back yelling **HOT**! After I repeated this demonstration several minutes he appeared to understand. Within a week he would pass by the oven, point to it and yell **HOT**! At less than a year old he understood that touching the oven could result in getting burned. I was truly amazed at how someone so young could associate the oven with pain.

However, what is even more amazing is the number of people who continue to make decisions with painful consequences. They know that unexcused absences could result in job termination, but they choose to miss work. They know that shoplifting is a crime and could result in a criminal record, but still choose to slip a pair of sunglasses in their jacket. They know that they don't have money in the bank, but they still use a credit card or write a bad check. Certainly, if a person less than a year old can distinguish between right and wrong, we too can learn the difference.

Remember: Find your thrills through means that won't ruin you personally or professionally.

Mission Possible

Make Your Life A Mission—Not An Intermission

Tom Cruise, the well-known actor, had starring roles in Mission Impossible and Mission Impossible II. One of my favorite Tom Cruise films is Jerry Maguire. The story involves a sports agent played by Cruise who initially does anything to obtain and retain clients. At some point he realizes there is more to life than money. He writes a personal mission statement that totally refocuses his priorities. Soon he is fired from the agency and forced to strike out on his own. Based on his new personal and business philosophy, he is only able to sign one client. The story ends triumphantly when his client leads his team to a Super Bowl victory. The turning point for Jerry Maguire was the personal mission statement.

A year before the release of Jerry Maguire a business article stirred me to develop my own personal mission statement. In doing so, I experienced a tremendous awakening. It caused me to focus on who I am. I now encourage everyone to develop their own personal mission statement to define who he or she is and their reason for being on the planet.

The guidelines below should help in developing your own mission statement:

1. There is no right or wrong personal mission statement. Whatever works for you is right for you.

2. Your mission statement should be short and to the point. A good rule of thumb is your mission statement should be able to be understood by a 12-year-old.

3. Your job is not your mission statement. Don't let what you do define who you are.

4. Your mission statement should change over time. As you grow older your circumstances will change and you will see the world differently.

5. Write your mission statement down and commit it to memory. Make sure your mission statement is always within reach.

A personal mission statement will force you to be accountable to the one person you should hold to the highest standards—yourself.

Remember: Do the things you always dreamed of doing NOW.

Put It In Writing

Until you put your goals on paper, you have intentions that are seeds without soil.

Imagine on Tuesday your fairy godmother appears and grants you a one-week, all expenses paid vacation to Rio de Janeiro. What's the catch? You must leave Wednesday morning. Your joy is suddenly tempered by the realization that you have dozens of things to do on Tuesday. Ninety-nine percent of us faced with this dilemma would immediately make a list of all we had to accomplish that day and, more than likely, we would accomplish the items on that list. The mere act of writing tasks down subconsciously makes them more important to you. So it is with our goals. If you are truly committed to reaching your goals, you need to write them down.

Back in 1957, there was a study completed on the graduating class of Yale. The study revealed only three percent of class members had clearly defined, written goals. A follow up study done 20 years later found that in terms of business success, that same three percent had accomplished more than their other classmates combined.

When I was 24 years old, I made a list of my life's goals. One of those goals was to be a facility manager by age 30. Although I had no experience in facility management, I preceded to work day by day to accomplish that goal. Surprisingly, I missed it by only two months. I am convinced that writing that goal down helped me accomplish it.

Write your goals down and place them in several key places so that you can see them every day. I keep a list of my goals in my wallet, in my desk drawer at work and on my nightstand so that I am constantly reminded of where I want to go in life and how I'm going to get there. I am convinced that writing that goal down helped me ultimately accomplish it.

Remember: So let it be written; So let it be done.

Watch The Ball

"The tragedy of life doesn't lie in not reaching your goals. The tragedy lies in not having any goals to reach."

Dr. Benjamin Mays

A s an avid golfer I am constantly looking for small adjustments that might help improve my swing. However, no matter how many adjustments I make to my swing, in order to hit the ball I must watch the ball. Similarly, it would be difficult for even the most skilled archer to hit a bull's eye if he was blindfolded. Focusing on the object we are trying to hit is critical in golf and archery, but even more essential in life.

Too many people expect to somehow reach their dreams without really focusing on them or developing a solid set of goals. In fact, researchers estimate that 95 percent of people in the United States do not have goals. Goals provide the road map for us to reach our dreams. Short and long term goals are important and necessary in all areas of our life including physical, professional, financial, spiritual, family, mental and social.

Just as we can't hit a target we can't see, we can't reach for goals we don't have. Isn't it about time you joined the five percent of us who do have goals? Start today by developing a set of realistic goals, write these goals down and place them where they can be seen every day.

Remember: Know where you are going or you might end up somewhere else.

Championship
Pointers

Lord grant that I may always desire more
than I can accomplish.

Unless you try something beyond what you have
already mastered you will never grow.

He who attempts the impossible
has little competition.

Handle Your Hurts

Things turn out best for those who make the best of the way things turn out.

John Wooden

It sometimes takes people a long time to realize that life is not fair. The longer we live the more adversity we will face. For some, adversity becomes a stumbling block. For others it becomes a stepping stone. One of the great examples of successfully handling adversity can be found in Abraham Lincoln. Consider his record:

Failed in business	1831
Defeated for Legislator	1832
Failed in business again	1833
Sweetheart died	1835
Suffered Nervous Breakdown	1836
Defeated for Congress	1843
Defeated for Senate	1855
Defeated for Vice President	1856
Defeated for Senate	1858
Elected President	1860

If Abraham Lincoln were alive today, he would have no chance of winning the Presidency because of his failed business experiences and clinical depression. But back then, he just kept reaching for his dream. Now he is recognized as one of our great presidents.

My mother-in-law has a favorite saying: "When life hands you lemons, make lemonade." Even a sour lemon can be turned into a sweet glass of lemonade. Whether you missed a key promotion, faced a critical illness or lost a loved one, recognize that disappointments are a fact of life and a catalyst for personal growth. If you want to make your dreams come true, look at all your negative experiences as opportunities to learn more about yourself and become a better person for having lived through them.

Remember: Those things that do not kill us make us stronger.

You Make Your Own Bed

Sometimes you help others by not helping them.

One of the most difficult and unpleasant tasks I face in my position is the termination of employees. The job becomes even more difficult when the employee has been with the organization for several years and has in some way contributed to its success. Although I agonize greatly over these decisions, it is my job to do what is best for the organization. I cannot allow personal feelings to influence my decisions.

When the time finally comes and it is apparent that the individual must be terminated, I always think back to my high school football coach. At the start of football season, he always said there were enough uniforms for everybody who chose to try out for the team. Therefore, no one had to be cut. All he asked is that each individual show up every day, work hard and contribute by supporting other players. These were simple guidelines for staying on the team. Unfortunately, there were always some that could not follow these guidelines and ultimately left or were dismissed.

Similarly, employees are given the same opportunity. The organization asks its individuals to work hard, contribute by being good team players and obey the rules set forth in employee manuals. After investing in training, benefits, and uniforms, most employers want their personnel to be long-term contributors. Unfortunately, some will not obey the guidelines prescribed. In essence, they terminate themselves.

As you reach your goals and become responsible for supervising others, keep in mind that personnel decisions have to be based on what's best for the organization. Your job is to provide an opportunity for people to be successful. The choice is then left up to the individual. Will he or she make it happen? If not, your only alternative is providing that opportunity for success to someone else.

Remember: It ain't easy being the boss.

Can You Get Me Some Tickets?

You can probably count your true friends on one hand.

In my business, people constantly ask me for complimentary tickets to events. Often I haven't heard from these people in years.

I learned early in my career that my access to tickets could be a problem. Thus, I rely on the words of a former boss, "Friends are friends, business is business." I have never allowed friends to get in the way of proper business decisions. Because the tickets are not mine, I am never in a position to give them away. Likewise, I do not feel it is my place to help friends meet celebrities, get jobs and acquire vendor contracts.

One of the things you realize is that true friends will not compromise your job by asking you for special favors. Because I view all other people as associates, I don't have any problem denying their request.

As my friend Otis once said, "If you never let the devil in the house, you never have to kick him out." Simply put, don't start helping associates with special favors, and you'll never have to worry about trying to stop. Certainly that does not mean that you cannot remain cordial with these individuals.

Remember: Take care of business by not taking care of friends.

You'll Never Make Enough

The amount of money you receive will always be in direct proportion to the demand for what you do, your ability to do it, and the difficulty of replacing you.

Earl Nightingale

There is a biblical parable in the book of Matthew about a man who hired several men to work in his vineyard at various times of the day. For those first hired, he settled on a penny for the day's work. He hired the others agreeing only to pay them a fair wage. At the end of the day, all of the men were paid a penny. At that point, the men first hired became angry believing they deserved more for working all day. The owner of the vineyard reminded them that he had done them no harm because they had agreed on a penny for a day's work. I often see the same kind of anger and jealously in employees who feel they should be paid more than their co-workers. In some cases, they have been employed longer. In other cases, they believe their job is more important. And in almost all cases, they believe they do a better job.

For reasons that are not always apparent, an employer must try to pay people equal wages. Certainly this is not always fair. **But life is not fair.** As is the case with the parable, the bottom line is that we accept a job at a certain rate of pay and that is all our employer owes us. Resentment for our employer and co-workers is counter-productive. The best way to make more money is to demonstrate, through your work, that you are an invaluable part of the organization.

Remember: The best reward is a job well done.

No Whining Allowed

The man who complains about the way the ball bounces is likely the one who dropped it.

O nce there was a young lady who joined an order of nuns that had a vow of silence. The nuns were, however, allowed to speak two words every ten years. After the first ten years the Mother Superior came to her and asked for her two words. The nun responded, "Food cold." Another ten years passed and the Mother Superior allowed her two more words. The nun responded, "Bed hard." Ten more years passed and the nun was allowed two more words. The nun responded, "I quit." The Mother Superior at that point said, "It's just as well. You've done nothing but complain since you've been here."

Almost all of us at one time or another have worked with someone who chronically complains—especially about his or her job. It makes you want to ask, "Why don't you get a job somewhere else?" Unfortunately, if you associate with these people long enough they can have a negative influence on your attitude.

If you find yourself dreading going to work in the morning and complaining about your job, you need to look carefully at what it is about the job you don't like. Is it the job responsibilities? Is it your co-workers? Is it your rate of pay? If you can't resolve these problems within yourself, it's probably time for you to seek employment elsewhere.

Remember: Attitude determines altitude.

Getting Better
Every Day

I don't think much of a man who is not wiser today
than he was yesterday.

Abraham Lincoln

One of life's greatest lessons was taught to me by Muggsy Bogues. Muggsy is the shortest person ever to
play in the NBA, at only five feet three inches tall.

Muggsy grew up in a low income housing area and each
day had to take the trash from his apartment to a dumpster down the street. He would also use this time to dribble his basketball. Each day, he would try to simultane-
ously empty the trash and dribble the ball. When he first
started, he would spill all the trash before reaching the
dumpster, prompting laughter from his neighbors.
Undaunted, he continued each day to take out the trash
and dribble the basketball. Over time he became quite

proficient and was able to even do trick dribbling while completing his chore. The key to his success was improving a little bit everyday.

Similarly, when I dared to run a 10K race with several friends, my initial training involved running one lap the first day, two laps the second day, three laps the third day and so on until I built up my endurance to complete the race.

If you are to reach your goals, you should develop a personal philosophy to improve every day of your life. I like to compare this to mountain climbing. Very seldom does the mountain climber have an opportunity to rest-he's either ascending or descending. Our challenge is to keep ascending, reaching one goal after another, climbing one mountain after another. Whether you learn a new word each day, run an extra quarter mile, or simply spend more time with your kids, you should strive to be better today than yesterday and better tomorrow than today.

Remember: The knowledge you gain today is the wisdom you keep for a lifetime.

Never Stop Learning

Never stop learning
Never stop growing
Never stop seeking the brightest star
Never stop moving from where you are

Never stop trying
Never stop reaching
Never stop doing what you can do
Never stop growing your whole life through

Children aren't the only ones
who should learn and grow
All of us have so much to learn
There's so much that we could know

Never stop learning
Never stop growing
Never stop seeking the brightest star
Never stop moving from where you are

What we learn is up to us
What we seek, we find
Never doubt what you have inside
All you need is in your mind

Put God First

With God all things are possible.

Matthew 19:26

As I hugged my grandmother before heading off for my freshman year of college, I will always remember the three words she whispered to me, "Put God first." My grandmother is one of the kindest people I know. She has shown me how fulfilling life can be through believing in and putting your trust in a higher power. Her words of wisdom have remained with me, and although I sometimes stumble, I have tried to keep God first in my life.

No matter what your religion, I believe attending weekly worship services is an important part of maintaining your faith. I am amazed at how many people profess to be religious yet never attend weekly worship services. I personally believe that just as success favors those who surround themselves with successful people, success in religion comes from surrounding ourselves with others who share our faith. To be a great basketball player you need to play with other great basketball players. You gain no competitive edge shooting hoops alone in your driveway. To be a world class musician, you need to play with other great musicians in a symphony. It doesn't do much good to sit at home playing your horn for your immediate family. An alcoholic's best chance to quit drinking usually involves joining AA or some other support group. It is very difficult to try to stop drinking on your own. In all three of these examples there is not much to be accomplished alone.

Whether sharpening basketball skills, playing beautiful music or breaking an addiction, being in the presence of others committed to the same goals brings out the best in people. Similarly, you can't sit at home and say a couple of prayers and replace the feeling of being around others who share your beliefs. This certainly does not mean that you can't be deeply committed to your religion if you don't attend worship services. I just believe that people need people. Whether you worship at a church, synagogue or mosque, make it a point to begin visiting your place of worship on a regular basis.

Remember: Don't let the hearse bring you to church.

Ripe For Picking

Good, Better, Best—Never Let It Rest. Until Your Good Is Better And Your Better Is Best.

E arly in my professional career I can remember having a discussion with my mentor. He said, "If you're green you're ripe, if you're red you're rotten." I reflected on that for a few minutes, but couldn't quite figure out its meaning. He explained that as an apple ripens, it is green in color. At some magical moment it will be red and perfect for eating. The problem is that the magical moment lasts just a short period of time and after it has passed, the apple stops growing, deteriorates and is no longer desirable for eating.

The illustration applies to us also. As we go through school, accept our first jobs, climb the career ladder and become professionals we must never forget that there is always more to learn. We should view each day we are blessed with as a school day—another learning opportunity.

If we ever get to a point where we feel we've grown as much as we need to, we will surely deteriorate and become rotten. It is important to make a personal commitment and a conscious effort to grow a little every day and never be satisfied.

Remember: Learning is a treasure that will follow its owner everywhere.

Winners Never Quit

It is hard to beat someone who never gives up.

Babe Ruth

Michael Jordan, one of the greatest basketball players of our time, is one of the greatest examples of never giving up. As a tenth grader, Michael was cut from his high school basketball team. That's right, the player who may be considered the greatest of all time was not good enough to make his high school basketball team. He was so hurt that he came home after school, closed the door to his room, and cried. When his mother finally came home, he told her what had happened and they cried together.

When asked about that experience Michael says, "It's probably good that it happened. It was good because it made me know what disappointment felt like. And I knew that I didn't want to have that feeling ever again."

Realizing he wanted to make the team the following season, Michael used that tenth grade year to refine his skills and improve his game. Needless to say, he made the team the next year, went on to the University of North Carolina where he played on a national championship team, and, then played for the Chicago Bulls where he won numerous championships. Just think if Michael had decided to give up on basketball that day and join the chess club or debate team, we would have lost one of our great national treasures. The point is Michael Jordan had a dream to make his high school team. That dream developed into a player who will probably be considered the greatest ever.

All of us deserve to reach our dreams. If you are to realize your dreams, you would do well to memorize a famous speech by Sir Winston Churchill. It consisted of these nine words, "**Never Give Up, Never Give Up, Never Give Up.**"

Remember: You only lose when you're willing to give up.

I Still Owe How Much?

How do you stop a wild elephant from charging?
You take away his credit cards.

Anonymous

Early in my career, I learned a valuable lesson about credit cards. Using my credit card, I purchased some bedroom furniture for $500.00. Because I was living paycheck to paycheck, I could only afford to pay the card company's $10 minimum for the first few months. After about 18 months, I still owed over $450.00—even though I had paid approximately $200.00 to the credit card company. After realizing it was going to take several more years to pay for my bedroom furniture, I decided to use my entire income tax refund check to pay off that debt. At that point, I made a commitment to only use credit cards for my reimbursable business expenses or emergencies. It certainly takes discipline, but my life and financial situation are much more stable.

Too often I hear people say, "I just can't get ahead."
Credit card debt is undoubtedly one of the primary factors contributing to this condition. Michael Knight, a
financial consultant stated in an article, "There are over a
billion credit cards in circulation in the United States ...
that's almost four cards for every American man, woman
and child." And nearly 70 percent of all credit card hold-
ers in the United States carry a revolving card balance
each month, i.e., they are paying the minimum amount
due. Consider this: By making minimum payments (two
percent of the balance or $10, whichever is greater) on a
balance of $1,000 with an annual interest rate of 18 per-
cent it will take more than 19 years to pay off the
account, and you will pay nearly $1,900 interest on that
$1,000.

Later in this book, I stress the importance of investing to
secure your future. Realize though, that you need to pay
off all your credit card debt before investing. After paying
off your credit card debt, cut up all those cards. You'll
never have such fun with a pair of scissors.

**Remember: If you can't pay cash for it, you don't
really need it.**

Socks Then Shoes

The ability to use your time well and concentrate is everything if you want to succeed in business—or in anything else for that matter.

Lee Iacocca

Several years ago, my boss began using a time management system incorporating a sophisticated day-timer. I and several other employees persuaded him to purchase the system for us, and within one month we realized how much it could improve our efficiency.

However, I soon found that too many other factors that I could not control impacted my time. I likened my situation to being the only doctor in a small town. He has a full schedule of patients, but also has to deal with every medical emergency. He is effective, but has very few routine days. While the time management system was worthwhile, I would be more productive if I relied on "**flexible planning**."

Flexible planning is a concept Charlie Jones speaks of in his book, *Life is Tremendous,* and is one of his seven principles of leadership. Very simply, flexible planning allows for the daily emergencies that invariably occur. By planning for these emergencies in your schedule, you never get upset or flustered when they happen.

If factors beyond your control impact your time at work, I encourage you to use a flexible planning system. Focus daily on those things that you absolutely have to accomplish. Make sure those things get done, and then move on to other items on your list as time allows. You will be more efficient and far less stressed.

Remember: Do all you can do. Then go home and sleep like a baby.

Integrity

If you have integrity, nothing else matters. If you don't have integrity, nothing else matters.

Alan Simpson

Most people who meet me are surprised to discover that my undergraduate degree is in criminal justice. I joke with them that my degree helps because as a facility manager I deal with a lot of crooks. Unfortunately the entertainment business often creates situations where event promoters sometimes have to be less than scrupulous in order to survive. The following story illustrates the point.

Several years ago we had a concert that evolved into a nightmare. The day started with the sound and lighting equipment arriving four hours late, throwing the whole production schedule behind. We decided to delay the concert by one hour. Just before the show started, we learned that one of the performers was not feeling well and might not be able to perform. Some of the performers also had a dispute over who should perform first. After a heated argument and firm persuasion on my part, the concert finally began and even though it was delayed, I believe most of the patrons were satisfied.

Not surprisingly, I was frustrated at the end of the night, not necessarily with the promoter, but with the day in general. Just before we said goodnight, the promoter offered his hand for a handshake. Neatly concealed in the palm of his hand were several $100.00 bills. Upon realizing his "peace" offering, I politely declined the money. I told him thanks, but I was just doing my job and the best way to thank me was to never let this happen again in my building. He understood and we have frequently worked together since that event.

The problem with taking money from people you do business with is that you never know when they might ask you for a favor that compromises your position. For that reason, never take money from someone for doing a job you are already paid to do.

Remember: Your integrity is something that cannot be taken away from you without your consent.

Championship Pointers

You can't be truly successful and dishonest.

A man of honor regrets a discreditable act even when it has worked.

Character is what you do when nobody is watching.

A clear conscience makes for a soft pillow.

Attitude Determines Altitude

People can alter their lives by altering their attitudes.

William James

Recently I had the opportunity to hear a human resources professional speak to a group of college students about different issues that could affect them as they entered the working world. One of the more interesting points she shared included her observation of valuable traits that great employees possess. The first one was a positive attitude followed by enthusiasm, high energy and competitive spirit.

Afterwards, I thought about what was said, reflecting on great employees I'd encountered over the years. Of all the great employees with which I've been associated, the one trait they shared was attitude. In fact, I believe the most important trait one can possess is attitude. If an employee has a great attitude, all other traits seem to fall into place.

A study by Harvard University revealed that 85% of the reasons for success, accomplishments, promotions, etc. were because of attitude and only 15% because of technical expertise. Charles Swindoll, author and pastor, once wrote, "The longer I live the more I realize the impact of attitude on life. Attitude to me is more important than facts. It is more important than the past, than education, than money, than circumstances, than failures, than successes, than what other people think or say or do. It is more important than appearance, ability, or skill."

Chick Hearn, the famous sportscaster echoed those same thoughts when he said, "there is one word which I feel controls everything we do. That word is ATTITUDE! It will bring us whatever we want, or will keep us from reaching any of our goals. Be assured, attitude will play an important role in any success you achieve."

Knowledge, experience, education and job skills don't mean anything if an employee can't get along with others, is a chronic complainer, and is generally unpleasant to have in the workplace. The person with a great attitude and a few technical skills is likely to get a job or promotion because skills can be taught while a bad attitude is very difficult to change. In short, attitude is more important than aptitude.

In life there are few things over which we truly have control. One of those things that we can control is our attitude. W. E. Henly, the poet, once wrote, "I am the master of my fate, the captain of my soul." You are captain of your soul and your ship. If you are to reach your dreams, you should strive to be known by your peers as a person with a **super** attitude.

Remember: You can complain because the roses have thorns, or rejoice because the thorns have roses.

Low Man On The Totem Pole

Always make the boss look good.

M ost young people in entry level positions after a few months on the job feel they know as much as their boss. It reminds me of the young man who turned 21 and said he couldn't believe how much his parents had learned in seven years. Obviously, as a 14 year old he thought he knew it all and his parents knew nothing. Similarly, young people just out of the academic world and feeling they can conquer the world honestly believe they could do their bosses' job much better. Later in their careers, after they become supervisors and begin taking on more responsibility and managing more people, they understand how naive they were a few years earlier.

Besides feeling they know as much as their boss, resentment also surfaces in young people when supervisors seem to get all the perks and benefits. For example, the boss decides to take a trip to Hawaii for a marketing convention and sends you to Tupelo, Mississippi for a seminar on time management. Not surprisingly, your boss hasn't worked in marketing, which is your specialty in over 10 years. Your supervisor gets a nice big fruit basket from a vendor at Christmas while you don't even get a Christmas card. Not surprisingly, you work closely with the vendor and you are probably the only reason he has the account. The boss gets interviewed by all three local TV stations and is even featured in a national publication for an innovative customer service program at your company. Not surprisingly, you conceived and implemented the program over a year ago. Unfortunately, these examples happen every day.

Fortunately, I have had great respect for all my supervisors and understood early on the principle of **R.H.P.** (**Rank Has Privileges**). Simply put, the one who has the most rank, seniority, or is the supervisor or owner of the business is able to call the shots and enjoy the benefits of his position. Realizing this early in your career can spare you a great deal of frustration and anger which is counterproductive. The boss having all the fun is not fair, but as a young person you should aspire to use RHP for yourself one day.

Remember: The vice president never gets shot.

Just The Facts

Tell the truth and you never have to remember anything.

Recently I read a story about a state senator who falsified information on his resume after finishing law school. While he campaigned for a U.S. House of Representatives seat, his falsified resume was discovered, attracting more attention than the issues affecting voters. Not surprisingly, he lost the election, but more importantly he lost his credibility. Reflecting on those events the former senator couldn't believe that he could have put such unnecessary emphasis on his political career.

According to a study by Werra and Associates, nearly 15 percent of top executives lie on their resumes about their education. It is easy to see how someone just finishing college with little experience would be tempted to falsify his or her resume to get that all important first job. After all, most of us preparing resumes have tried to cast ourselves in the best possible light. But trying to make yourself look advantageous is different from misrepresenting your qualifications, educational achievements and abilities.

As is the case with the state senator, even small misrepresentations can come back to haunt you later in your business career and destroy your credibility. For that reason, use your resume to make yourself look as good as possible, but never misrepresent your abilities.

Remember: No job is worth sacrificing your credibility.

Career Planning or Job Hunting

The grass may look greener on the other side but it still has to be mowed.

Throughout my life, I have benefited from several significant personal relationships, two of which immediately come to mind. The first relationship involved my boss and mentor when I started my career in public service. Although he was an older white gentleman and I was a young black kid, we were friends from the beginning. Like all good mentors he saw more in me than I saw in myself. As he taught me about my profession and life in general, we formed a father-son relationship and I still communicate with him regularly. One of the things I learned from him was the value of job dedication. This gentleman worked for the same organization for over thirty years. He could have moved to other jobs and made more money, but he remained loyal to that organization.

His loyalty was rewarded as he is now retired, enjoying a comfortable life and a considerable monthly pension.

By contrast, my other notable relationship involves a young man I met several years ago when I spoke to his ninth grade class. I took an interest in him and became his big brother, offering friendship, advice and guidance. Today he has grown into a fine young man. In the years after finishing community college he has moved to several jobs. He always manages to move up in pay, but never stays more than a few months on any particular job. While this may seem like a profitable career path to him, I believe it is better to remain with an organization for at least two or three years.

By not staying with an organization for two years or more, you might sacrifice the opportunity for promotions and ultimately, increased salary. By working at a company for several years you also demonstrate stability in your life. Thus, perspective employers will be more likely to hire you and invest money in your training.

If you do change jobs frequently, I recommend two things. First, become skilled at resume preparation. Secondly, develop your own retirement savings plan. If you don't, you'll have to work all your life because you'll never stay at one company long enough to draw a pension.

Remember: Good things come to those who wait.

What Good Are You To Me?

If you are not part of the solution, you are part of the problem.

By working in a supervisory position for several years, I have learned the value of dedicated employees and had the opportunity to work with several people who have been invaluable to me and the organization we serve. Along with superior attitudes, technical knowledge, loyalty and commitment they offer our organization, these individuals possess another attribute that makes them invaluable to the "boss." This attribute is the ability to assist in solving organizational problems.

The most valuable employees are the ones who not only clearly outline a problem, but offer suggestions for resolving the problem. Although my position requires that I am responsible for solving problems, I do not have all the answers. By thinking about our mission, our employees usually suggest several solutions for a problem and present what they believe is the best one. In the majority of cases, their thoughts match my own.

If you want to be an asset to your boss, think through problems and develop possible solutions before you present them to him or her. You'll save everyone time, which is their most valuable asset.

Remember: Being labeled a problem solver is the best label you can have.

Just Sign On The Dotted Line

Don't sign your life away.

O ne of the ways I try to inspire young professionals is to share some of my own professional experiences. This one almost cost me my career.

When I started out as an assistant facility manager, I was always quite busy. My responsibilities included booking, personnel administration, public relations, marketing and event coordination, plus I signed purchase orders.

One particularly busy day, my chief engineer brought a purchase order into my office for the repair of some exterior windows. All I noticed on the form was a figure of $1,950 in the right hand column. I signed the form without asking any questions and continued with my work. You can imagine my surprise when my boss called me into his office to ask why I had signed a purchase order for $93,000. If I had read the form carefully, I would have noticed the column on the purchase order which stated "quantity." Unaware, I had signed repairs for 48 of those exterior windows at $1,950 each. Although the engineer did not point out the amount of the purchase order, the error was my fault for not taking time to read the details.

After chastising me for the problem I had created, my boss bailed me out. Fortunately, I had a supportive boss. Otherwise, I probably would have lost my job because money for that repair was not in the budget. Needless to say I have never signed another document, either professional or personal, without knowing exactly what I am signing.

In your professional and personal dealings, I encourage you to read documents thoroughly before signing them. If you don't feel comfortable with what you are signing, obtain professional assistance as needed and don't sign the documents until you do feel comfortable. From purchase orders at work to automobile purchase agreements to contracts for an apartment or new home, make sure you read and understand all items in the documents before signing them. We've all heard the expression **Reading is Fundamental**. This expression is never more appropriate than as it relates to reading important documents.

Remember: Always look before you leap.

In Search Of Excellence

Pursue perfection, accept excellence.

H. Jackson Brown, Jr.

The great civil rights leader and statesman Martin Luther King once said, "If it falls your lot to be a street sweeper, sweep streets as Raphael painted pictures, sweep streets as Michelangelo carved marble, sweep streets as Beethoven composed music, or Shakespeare wrote poetry." The great football coach Vince Lombardi once said, "The quality of a person's life is in direct proportion to their commitment to excellence." A guy I met while visiting the Bahamas said, "It's not what you do, it's how you do it."

All three of these men defined excellence. Whatever job you undertake, it should be your goal to do your best.

Throughout my athletic career, I learned the value of sacrifice, discipline, dedication and hard work. All of these qualities contribute to excellence in any endeavor. You may not always be the best, but you can always strive to do your best.

Remember: Excellence can only be measured by the standards you set for yourself. Only you know whether you did the best you could.

Championship Pointers

Leaders take responsibility and give credit.

Remember the difference between a boss
and a leader.
A boss says, "Go"—A leader says "Let's Go."

The buck stops here.

When in charge, take charge!.

Exceed Expectations

The harder you work the luckier you get.

I had the opportunity to hear General Colin Powell
speak shortly after he had retired from active duty in
the armed forces. He had risen to the rank of four-star
general and become the first African-American to sit on
the Joint Chiefs of Staff. I will never forget his answer to
the question, "How were you able to become so successful?" He affirmed, "I worked like a dog for 28 years."

Another great example of a hard worker is a basketball
player named Spud Webb. At 5'7," he was one of the
shortest players in the National Basketball Association. In
his book, *Flying High*, he says that during the summers of
his high school career, he would begin playing in the
morning and often played right through lunch. He would
always come home for dinner and watch an hour of TV.
Then he would go back to the courts until dark and, on
some evenings, come home and put flashlights in the trees

in order to keep shooting baskets.

This emphasizes that it takes more than talent to make it to the NBA. Such distinction also requires hard work. Basketball legend Magic Johnson summed it up nicely, saying, "Talent is never enough. With few exceptions; the best players are also the hardest workers."

If you are to reach the top of your chosen profession, you must be willing to work harder than your competition. The sacrifice involved in reaching the top is not easy but, if it were easy everybody would be doing it.

Remember: The only place success comes before work is in the dictionary.

It's A "J" Not A "G"

A person's name is to that person the sweetest and most important sound in any language.

Dale Carnegie

As a person who has a different spelling of a fairly common last name, I am constantly reminding people that my last name is spelled with a J instead of a G. I have even had instances where I spelled my name to someone on the phone and still received correspondence with my name spelled incorrectly.

Nothing irritates me more than receiving correspondence (particularly from people selling products or seeking employment) with my name spelled wrong. It seems to show a total lack of respect for me because the writer didn't care enough to check the correct spelling of my name. Needless to say, I place this correspondence to the side or in the trash.

Correspondence with the wrong title represents another example of someone not practicing professional courtesy. Although I was promoted to my current position several years ago, I still receive letters with my former title.

In business, you can't afford to make mistakes. For that reason, practice these simple rules:

1. **Always know the correct spelling of names.**
2. **Always know the proper title.**
3. **Always know the correct pronunciation of names.**
4. **Always use the individual's title if you use your own.**

Remember that people's names are one of the few things that set them apart from all other individuals in the world. You know how important your name is to you. Show others the courtesy of getting theirs right.

Remember: You only get one chance to make a first impression.

Can You Spare Some Change?

A penny saved is a penny earned.

One evening while contemplating my daughter's future and the staggering potential cost of her college education, I came up with a profitable idea. I noticed how much spare change my wife and I had lying around on our dresser. It occurred to me that if we both deposited this change in a safe place on a daily basis, it would not take long to accumulate.

We went out and bought four big piggy banks, one for each coin (quarters, dimes, nickels and pennies) and placed them in my daughter's room so that we could see them daily. Each day we deposit our change in the appropriate bank, averaging $1.50 per day. We've become so conscious of this savings vehicle that when shopping we go out of our way to get extra change. The best part is we never miss the money.

Our goal is to count the change on our daughter's birthday (December 24) each year, roll it up and take it to the bank. We'll then take the savings and invest it in an interest-bearing account. We hope through our change fund and cash gifts from relatives and friends to save at least $1,000 per year. That sum invested wisely for 18 years should return a sizable sum of money. It probably won't be enough for her entire college education, but it will certainly help out.

Young professionals would be wise to use this change fund as a painless way to start their investment portfolios. First, put something aside every day. Second, commit to making your change fund a long-range investment. With compound interest if you saved just a dollar a day starting at age 20 and invested it wisely, you would have over $500,000 at age 65. Finally, as your income increases, contribute more to your change fund. If you start with a dollar a day at age 25, move up to two dollars a day by age 27 and five dollars a day by age 30. Your change fund can even double as a "rainy day" fund for life's emergencies. Start today and you'll be surprised how much you have this time next year.

Remember: Money is only important when you don't have any.

Money In The Bank

I've been rich and I've been poor. Rich is better.

As a young person in my twenties living paycheck to paycheck, it was difficult for me to imagine that I might one day want to retire. Now, after many years of working and being a parent, I not only look forward to retirement, I want to retire in my mid-fifties. Over the last five years, I have studied many financial self-help books and implemented some personal strategies that should allow me to reach my goal.

It's interesting that a majority of young professionals don't plan to die, yet also don't plan to live. Most young people would probably tell you they expect to live at least into their seventies. But if you asked this same group what they are doing financially to live comfortably and independently at that age, they would probably say, "nothing."

All of the financial self-help books I have read make the

same point. Time and money work together to create wealth. The following illustration explains the equation. If you invest $2,000 in a tax-deferred retirement account each year between the ages of 20 and 25 and never invest another dime, you will have more money when you reach age 65 than if you wait until you are 25 and invest $2,000 each year for the next 40 years in the same account, at the same rate of return. This is accomplished by the magic of compound interest. (Don't ask me how, but it works).

The message is clear. You need to start saving for retirement now. Then you can look forward to the future with confidence.

Remember: You're never too young to start saving for retirement.

It's My Party

How old would you be if you didn't know how old you was?

Satchel Paige

Anyone who is close to me knows of my great love for kids. They offer such exceptional potential and energy that I become inspired just being around them. A few years ago, I decided to start hosting a birthday party for myself and invite only kids. What started as a small affair with nieces, nephews and my friends' children grew into a major event with over 25 guests, none over 12 years old. I held the party at a family fun center complete with pizza, ice cream, cake, video games, go carts and bumper boats. Most importantly, I allowed myself to have as much fun as the kids.

I was often asked why I threw this annual party for children only. First of all, they give the best gifts—their smiles. Secondly they keep me feeling young. Finally, the birthday party reminds me never to take myself too seriously.

Although I'm over 35 years old I still feel youthful. I'm physically active, playing racquetball or basketball at least three times per week. I watch what I eat (despite an occasional banana split and a little too much caffeine in soft drinks). I tell people I'm planning to live to be 100 years old. Sure I might not make it. But remember—those who fail to plan, plan to fail.

Too often our family, friends and co-workers try to make us feel (or at least act) our age. They say things like, "I just noticed all your gray hair," or "You aren't as fast as you used to be." All of these statements may be true, but they shouldn't make us feel any less alive or good about ourselves. I welcome some gray hairs and laugh lines. After all, I earned them. And if you feel like a kid at heart, you'll never grow old.

Remember: You are only as old (or young) as you feel.

Love Is Spelled
T-I-M-E

Too much love never spoils children. Children become spoiled when we substitute presents for presence.

One of the greatest days of my life was my second Father's Day. After I took my wife and daughter to church, we spent a few hours at home and the rest of the afternoon at Carowinds amusement park. That evening I gave my daughter her bath and read her a bedtime story. Finally, she fell asleep. Most of my Sundays include a few hours on the golf course, so initially I was disappointed I had not been able to play golf on Father's Day. That lost opportunity turned out to be a blessing in disguise.

I received a couple of nice gifts that day, but the best gift I received happened later that night. Almost every night my daughter would wake up and need to be comforted back to sleep. After she learned to talk, she always called out for her mother. On that night she called out for daddy. Needless to say, my heart was warmed when I heard her call for me. As I recall that day, I am convinced that spending so much time with my daughter had a direct bearing on her calling out for me. Since then I have tried to spend even more time with her, not only quality time, but quantity time.

Similarly, our relationships with family and friends can be strengthened tremendously by investing more time in them. What would mean more to a friend: driving three hours to attend his mother's funeral or sending flowers? What would mean more to your cousin: having you attend her wedding or buying her a nice piece of china? What would mean more to a child: spending an hour with Michael Jordan or Michael Jordan donating $50,000 to a playground near that child's home? I believe the answer in all three of these examples is the gift of time. It means much more than all other gifts.

Remember: Your time is the greatest gift you have, give it to those you love as much as possible.

Little Children Follow Me

A careful man I must be,
Little children follow me.
I do not dare go astray,
For they will go the self-same way.

I cannot escape their watchful eye,
Whatever they see me do, they try.
Like me they say they're going to be,
Little children who follow me.

I must remember as I go,
Through summer suns and winter snows,
As I am building, for the years to be,
That little children follow me.

Unknown

If I Had My Child To Raise Over Again...

If I had my child to raise all over again,
I'd do less correcting and more connecting.
I'd take my eyes off my watch and watch with my eyes.
I would care to know less and know to care more.
I'd take more hikes and fly more kites.
I'd stop playing serious and seriously play.
I'd run through more fields and gaze at more stars.
I'd do more hugging and less tugging.
I would be firm less often and affirm much more.
I'd build self-esteem first and the house later.
I'd teach less about the love of power, and more about
the power of love.

Diane Loomans

The Living Saint

All of us have the capacity for greatness, because all of us have the ability to serve.

Martin Luther King Jr.

As a facility manager, I am often asked by people if I get to meet all the stars that come to the Coliseum. I have had the privilege of meeting some notable people, and always tried to use that moment as an opportunity to welcome these individuals and thank them for visiting our facility.

Celebrities I have met include President Bill Clinton, John McEnroe, Jimmy Connors, Garth Brooks, President Ronald Reagan, Billy Joel, Jesse Jackson, Michael Jordan and Don King. Probably the most excited I have been about meeting one of these famous people was during the 1994 Final Four when President Clinton visited our building. Having the opportunity to meet the standing president was unbelievable. By shaking his hand I felt that I had truly touched greatness.

That experience was unmatched until Mother Teresa visited our facility. Having been Catholic all my life, the event was especially memorable for me. After she left the stage, I was within arm's length of her. Before she got into her vehicle, she passed out some special commemorative medals. She handed me two of those medals which I will always cherish and hope to give to my two children some day. Although I didn't meet her, just touching the hand of a living saint was remarkable.

On that day, Mother Teresa talked about her ministry saying many things that other people have said before, however hearing it from her, I trusted that she lived her life every day serving God by serving others. Two things she said I shall always remember. First, we should try to help the poorest of the poor. Second, it's not what you do, it's the amount of love you put into what you are doing. Together, these two suggestions provide us with a simple equation for service to others. Find someone in our society who is neglected (the poor) and try to help them out (love them). Certainly we may not be able to match the contributions of Mother Teresa but we can all make a difference.

Remember: If it is to be, it's up to me.

No Problem Mon

It takes rain and sunshine to make a rainbow.

If you've ever visited the Bahamas you know that Bahamian people are some of the happiest, friendliest, most easy-going people you will ever meet. On my second trip to Nassau I recall being disappointed one morning because it appeared that rain would ruin my day of sightseeing. Looking out a hotel lobby window I asked a native if he thought it would rain all day. He responded, "It's no problem mon. That's just liquid sunshine; it will be gone shortly." Sure enough within a few minutes the rain had passed, and it turned out to be a beautiful day.

There are a lot of people who let the weather dictate the kind of day they are going to have. When it rains they mope around. When it's cold, they bundle up and become reclusive. When it's hot, they complain and become irritable. You would think that these people could move to a tropical paradise, and still have problems with the weather.

I can think back to the day my daughter arrived. It was a cold, rainy, snowy day, but in my eyes and heart it was sunny and 70 degrees. Nothing could have put a damper on that special day. Undoubtedly, you can think back to a special day in your life when the weather was miserable. Maybe it was the day you got married or the day your child was born. Whatever the occasion, it was special in spite of the weather.

Remember: You cannot change the weather, so make up your mind to cherish each day and you'll always have a "sunny" disposition.

It Was The Best
of Times

Today is the first day of the rest of your life.

Imagine an alien landing on our planet just in time to watch the 6:00 evening news. Within 10 minutes this stranger would think he had landed in the darkest corner of the galaxy. That's because the first 10 minutes of the broadcast is plagued by bad news, making one think these are the worst times in history.

Unfortunately, newspapers and magazines can be equally bad. This editorial from a prominent magazine characterizes our state of affairs. "We've got a huge deficit, major environmental problems, several social ills and so on. And these are serious problems. Unfortunately, we'll always have serious problems. However, equating "serious" with fatal would be to greatly underestimate this country. It is a gloomy moment in history...never has the future seemed so dark and incalculable. The United States is beset with racial, industrial and commercial chaos, drifting we know not where. Of our troubles no man can see the end." This editorial is right on target. The interesting thing is that it appeared in *Harpers* magazine in 1947. How can it be that an editorial written over 50 years ago appears to have been written last month? Because it is human nature to assume that these are the worst of times when, in fact, they are the best of times.

Consider all the technological and medical advances that are available to us today. Personal computers, cellular telephones, fax machines and the Internet provide information literally at the speed of light. New cures for diseases and healthcare programs allow us to live longer, healthier lives.

It is definitely one of the most exciting times in history to be alive. Yet we are constantly bombarded by media reports of doom and gloom because, unfortunately, good news does not intrigue the public. Therefore, if magazines, newspapers and television stations are to stay in business, they must report "bad news." How do you keep a positive outlook? Refuse to accept the naysayers' information. No matter what you hear on the news, these *are* the best of times.

Remember: It's All Good.

You Can't Get There From Here

Go confidently in the direction of your dreams.

Henry David Thoreau

A few years ago there was a joke in the Southeastern United States that said if you were going to hell, you had to catch a connecting flight in Atlanta. With the way airline hubs are situated this may not be far from the truth. You might leave Charlotte and fly to Pittsburgh to get to San Diego. Obviously, it would be faster to fly directly to San Diego, but with limited direct flights, the trip through Pittsburgh may be the only option.

One of my friends loves helping people achieve their dreams. She told me of a young lady she was counseling who was very focused on her career objective. The only problem was she only wanted to reach that career objective in Dallas, Texas. My friend told her, "Sometimes you must go through Chicago to get to Dallas." Unfortunately, this young lady had told several co-workers and supervisors of her dream to move to Dallas. No doubt she missed out on potential jobs because people thought she would only accept employment in Dallas.

If you really want to reach your dreams, you will have to make sacrifices. Although I am a true Tar Heel (a North Carolina native), I realized in order to be exposed to one of the best Sports Management Master's Degree programs in the country I had to spend a year in Massachusetts. The winter there was cold and the snow was deep, but I continued to mark the calendar and focus on my dream. And while I have no desire to ever live in New England again, I am grateful for my year in Massachusetts and the opportunities gained through my degree.

As you focus on your dreams and your ultimate destination, I encourage you not to restrict yourself geographically and give an advantage to your competition because you want to live in a certain city or part of the country. Even though a great job may not be in your favorite city, look at it as a career opportunity and connecting flight to your final destination.

Remember: Sometimes you have to take a detour to get where you want to go.

Communicate

God gave you two ears and one mouth. Listen twice as much as you talk.

Having been married for many years, I am often asked what it takes to stay together with your mate. I always say that it takes a lot of hard work and, more importantly, lots of communication. The following anecdote illustrates the importance of communication in a relationship.

As a facility manager I am always interested in visiting other arenas to see any other unique or innovative ideas that might be applicable to our facility. One year I had the opportunity to visit Orlando to watch Charlotte's arena football team play the Orlando Predators. I was to leave on Friday morning and return on Sunday afternoon.

About a week before leaving I mentioned the trip to my wife. Because of our work schedules we often did not see each other except briefly in the evenings. Without mentioning anything else about the trip, I packed my bags after she had gone to sleep on Thursday night. On Friday morning I woke before her and dressed comfortably for my flight. She woke briefly and asked if I was playing golf that day, to which I said, "Yes." I did play golf that day—in Orlando.

Needless to say, my wife forgot about the trip and was furious when I finally called at 11:00 on Friday night. We look back on this incident now and laugh, but I assure you at the time it was no laughing matter.

A lot of times, as relationships mature, couples stop communicating. When you think about it, the best times in your relationship were early on when you didn't need any other entertainment but each other. Remember when you could spend several hours just talking, either in person or by telephone? Relationships built on that foundation are sure to keep going strong for a long time.

Remember: If you want to rekindle the fire in your relationship, make communication your number one priority.

Walk Softly And Carry A Big Stick

You can never live a perfect day until you do something for someone who could never repay you.

John Wooden

Based on Coach Wooden's philosophy I believe my father lived a lot of perfect days. It was not until my father's death that I realized how great a man he was. So many people told me he had made a difference in their lives.

After several successful public service jobs, my father was encouraged by friends to run for the N.C. House of Representatives. He won six consecutive terms and was a very influential legislator at the time of his death. As chairman of the Health and Human Resources Committee his focus was helping all the undeserved and disenfranchised citizens of the state. Children, senior citizens and the disabled were the ones who benefited most from his desire to make a difference. The numerous posthumous honors he has received serve as a testament to how much he was loved. In fact, three years after his death an elementary school in my hometown was renamed for my dad.

When I looked through his personal papers I found an excerpt from one of his favorite plays. The play is entitled "The Cocktail Party" and was written by T.S. Eliot. It reads, "Half the harm that is done in this world is due to people who want to feel important." Marian Wright Edelman, president of the Children's Defense Fund followed the same line of thinking when she said, "Wanting to feel important is all right if it is not at the expense of doing important deeds." My father never cared about feeling important or receiving any credit for his work. For that reason, it is probably best that all of his honors came after his death.

As you go about the business of making a difference, I encourage you to do so quietly. After seeing how my father operated, I have adopted a personal philosophy of trying to let my actions speak for themselves. Mrs. Edelman sums it up best with the following quote, "You can achieve much in life if you don't mind doing the work and giving others the credit. You know what you do and the Lord knows what you do and that's all that matters."

Remember: Actions speak louder than words.

Championship Pointers

There is no limit to what a man can do or where he can go if he doesn't mind who gets the credit.

Who hath not served cannot command.

But the greatest among you shall be your servant.

We make a living by what we get—we make a life by what we give.

You Thought You Had It Bad

"From the time you are born til they carry you away in the hearse, nothing is so bad as it couldn't get worse."

Smokey Robinson

We all have heard about the man who felt sorry for himself because he had no shoes until he saw another man who had no feet. The moral of the story is we should rejoice in all the blessings we have.

Shortly after the first semester of my year in graduate school at the University of Massachusetts, my car was stolen. As a southern boy, the prospect of trudging through snow was not comforting, but realizing I could not bring the car back, I decided to remain positive and focus on obtaining my master's degree. At the time, one of my classmates who happened to hail from North

Carolina said if his car had been stolen he would have quit school and gone back home. I don't doubt he was telling the truth. Adversity is something we will face on a continual basis. In our families, jobs, relationships or organizations, there will always be situations that test us.

Next time you face adversity, consider three things. First, no matter how bad it seems, it could be worse. Second, any situation presents an opportunity to learn something. Finally, never let a bad situation keep you from being the most positive person you know.

Remember: Once you're down the only direction you can go is up.

Animal Trainers

Someone else's perception of you does not have to become your reality.

Les Brown

Someone once told me that fleas can be trained by placing them in a jar with a lid on top. After repeatedly attempting to jump out of the jar and hitting the lid, these insects will only jump so high. In fact, the lid can be removed, and they will still only jump high enough to avoid another headache.

I have witnessed the same conditioning of elephants in the circus. While not performing, these animals are held in their tents by a small chain attached to a stake and to one of their feet. It is amazing that these animals, some of which weigh in excess of 20,000 pounds, will stay in place. That's because when they were young, they had a chain attached to one of their feet and although they tried to escape, they were just not strong enough. Consequently, no matter how big elephants become, as long as they see that chain attached to their feet they don't believe they can go anywhere.

In both examples, these creatures have accepted the limitations imposed by their trainers. Many of us have similarly allowed ourselves to become influenced by our own personal trainers. What sets us apart from the animals is our ability to think and to know that we can break the chains that others put on us.

Remember: Others can stop you temporarily, but only you can stop you permanently.

Right Under My Nose

I am only one, but I am one; I can't do everything, but I can do something; what I can do, I ought to do, and by the grace of God, I will do.

A few years ago I attended a convention in San Diego. When I called for hotel reservations, I was surprised to hear the receptionist answer the phone, "**Hello, it's another beautiful day in San Diego**." I was skeptical that every day could be beautiful. Once I arrived in the city, I found that every day was, in fact, beautiful.

One of the highlights of that trip was a visit my wife and I took to Mexico. Late one night, we boarded a train across from our hotel and within 15 minutes we were at the Mexican border. We were both unprepared for what we would experience once we crossed the border. Although neither of us had ever traveled to a third world country, we immediately had a sense of what one must be like. We took a taxi to downtown Tijuana. As we exited the taxi, small children surrounded us selling trinkets and begging for money. It was a sight that I shall never forget. As I reflect on that trip, it is amazing that within 15 minutes we went from enjoying life in a metropolitan city to witnessing something that was truly disheartening and disturbing.

For those of us who live in major urban areas, we too can experience a similar contrast in lifestyles. All we have to do is get in our automobiles and drive no more than 15 minutes away from our cozy apartments or homes to a low income housing project in our city. Although young kids might not surround our vehicles and beg for money, we would find young people who go to sleep hungry at night, who sleep in the same bed with several siblings and whose parents have no hope of improving their circumstances in the foreseeable future.

I had the pleasure of starting a summer reading program for underprivileged kids a few years ago. Some co-workers and I devoted several hours a week to this project and felt we gained more out of the program than the kids because it made us understand how fortunate we are.

If you need to be reminded of your blessings, I encourage you to venture out of your neighborhood and into your surrounding community. I guarantee you won't have to go far to find someone who needs your help.

Remember: Charity begins at home.

Your Rent Is Due

Service is the rent we pay for being on this earth.

Marion Wright Edelman

My life has been touched by three great humanitarians who have shown me what it means to dedicate yourself to making a difference in the lives of others. The first is my great aunt Lula. After retiring as a public school teacher she worked tirelessly to serve others. She would spend time in the hospital comforting sick friends. She also tutored high school students and coordinated senior citizen activities.

A second influence in my life is my mother-in-law, Charity. As her name implies she is always giving. Although she never finished high school, she rose to the chairmanship of the county school board. She is so popular that she won a seat on the county board of commissioners on a campaign budget of $300.00. Her mission in life is to provide the best quality of life for the citizens of the county. She worked on the volunteer rescue squad for 25 years, and has started support groups for lupus victims and grieving parents. In 1994, she received the prestigious Susan B. Reynolds Award for a lifetime of community service.

Finally, my father, who served the citizens of North Carolina in the State House of Representatives, equally served as a tremendous inspiration to me. His efforts helped the disabled, senior citizens, and children. The purpose of the legislation he proposed was to help those who couldn't help themselves.

As I look at these three individuals they all have one thing in common: their desire to make a difference in the lives of others. Aunt Lula gave me this simple guide to live by:

If you want to be happy for an hour, take a nap.

If you want to be happy for a day, go fishing

If you want to be happy for a week, take a vacation.

If you want to be happy for a lifetime, serve others.

Compensation

I'd like to think when life is done
That I had filled a needed post,
That here and there I'd paid my fare
With more than idle talk and boast,
That I had taken gifts divine
The breath of life and manhood fine,
And tried to use them now and then
In service for my fellow men.

I'd hate to think when life is through
That I had lived my round of years
A useless kind, that leaves behind
No record in this veil of tears;
That I had, wasted all my days,
By treading only selfish ways,
And that this world would be the same
If it had never known my name.

I'd hate to think that here and there,
When I am gone, there shall remain
A happier spot that might have not
Existed had I toiled for gain;
That someone's cheery voice and smile
Shall prove that I had been worthwhile;
That I had paid with something fine
My debt to God for life divine.

Edgar A. Guest

Presentations by
Adonis "Sporty" Jeralds

CHAMPION
A motivational seminar designed for individuals seeking greater fulfillment in their professional lives. Developed from the book, *The Champion In You,* this presentation reveals the secret to attaining success while maintaining personal satisfaction.

MISSION POSSIBLE
A two-part interactive seminar created for individuals who want to take control of their lives through the development of goals and the creation of personal mission statements.

MENTORING begins with ME
What will be your legacy? This seminar challenges individuals to make a difference in the lives of others by taking an active role in helping others to live their dreams.

SUPERHERO
This inspirational presentation empowers individuals to believe, achieve and realize that everyone can live their dreams. Everyone can be a SUPERHERO.

For more information, or to book a presentation,
please contact:

Adonis "Sporty" Jeralds
P.O. Box 19773
· Charlotte, NC 28219
e-mail: sjeralds@aol.com
phone: (704) 541-1096
fax: (704) 544-6452
www.championinyou.com